William Andrew Leonard

Music in the western church

A lecture on the history of psalmody

William Andrew Leonard

Music in the western church
A lecture on the history of psalmody

ISBN/EAN: 9783742861474

Manufactured in Europe, USA, Canada, Australia, Japa

Cover: Foto ©Lupo / pixelio.de

Manufactured and distributed by brebook publishing software (www.brebook.com)

William Andrew Leonard

Music in the western church

MUSIC
IN THE
WESTERN CHURCH.

A LECTURE ON

THE HISTORY OF PSALMODY,

ILLUSTRATED WITH EXAMPLES OF THE

Music of the Various Periods.

BY

WILLIAM A. LEONARD.

LONDON: F. PITMAN, PATERNOSTER ROW.
BRISTOL: W. & F. MORGAN, CLARE STREET.

1872.

[*Entered at Stationers' Hall.*]

INTRODUCTION.

If the power of Song be such that it compelled the enemies of the Great Religious Movement in the sixteenth century to exclaim, "Luther has done us more harm by his songs than by his sermons," it cannot be uninteresting to trace its rise and growth in the Western Church.

Few, perhaps, who listen to the Anthem, or themselves join in the Hymn, ever ask, "Were these things always so?" A little reflection would, of course, convince them that Psalmody, like all other things, must have had a beginning—and a history. The Tunes of the present day are very different from those of the last century, and these again were unlike those of the preceding. For instance, it is but in comparatively late years that the Air, or Melody, has been given to the upper or Treble part; and it is certainly only in modern times that proper attention has been paid in the Church to the setting of Words to such Music as would best show forth their meaning; for the notes should, as Luther said, "Give Life to the Text."

The Author of the following pages is not unmindful of, nor would he deny the obligation he has been under to, the labours of such men as Mr. John Hullah, Dr. Rimbault, Rev. Henry Allon, and others, in this particular field of inquiry; but nevertheless he believes the present is the first attempt to give in a popular style, a history of the various stages of Psalmody in the Western Church.

The Rev. Henry Allon's lecture, "Music in relation to Church life," given some years ago on behalf of the London Young Men's Christian Association, is the nearest approach to such a history that the Author remembers to have seen. Mr. Allon's lecture, however, is not only incomplete but misleading; little or no mention is made of Descant, while the Gregorian Tones are presented with modern harmonies, whereas the merest tyro in musical history must know these Tones were always sung in unison (and are to this day in the Roman Catholic Church, except on special occasions), the employment of harmony being but of recent date. Anachronisms like this must, of course, greatly militate against the historical value of any work.

Dr. Rimbault, in papers contributed to "The Choir," in 1866, mostly confines himself to an account of the various Psalters published in this country, and does not give any musical illustrations.

Mr. Hullah, in his two series of Lectures on Music, takes in the whole field; his volumes are rendered doubly interesting by the examples taken from the works of various composers, and many of which are here published, he tells us, for the first time. In such a general survey, however, it was impossible to dwell minutely on any *one* of the many subjects which must have occurred to him, and the student who searches there for a history of Psalmody will search in vain.

Burney and Hawkins wrote still more pretentious Histories of Music, but their books are of little interest save to the theoretical musician.

The histories of Schlüter and Kiesewetter are more generally readable, because less technical.

A History of Music in the Western Church can indeed be only compiled after a careful perusal and comparison, not only of the works just enumerated, but also of the various Service Books and Psalters that have been published in bye-gone days. This the Author has striven to do thoughtfully and accurately; and he now offers the result of his labours to that "great congregation" who, as worshippers of the Almighty, weekly respond to the appeal of the Psalmist —" Let the people praise Thee, O God; yea, let *all* the people praise Thee."

For much valuable information relating to the

counter-tenor voice, as well as for an account of English song, the Author is indebted to some contributions of the Rev. W. F. Callaway to the "Tonic Sol-fa Reporter;" this gentleman has also rendered good service in reading music written in the old keys, as well as furnishing the writer with the result of his efforts to discover the system under which the Ambrosian and Gregorian Tones were first arranged.

To simplify matters, the musical examples are all given in the G and F cleffs, and on a stave of five lines; while for the convenience of those who cannot readily play from a full vocal score, a *compressed* score is added.

Marbeck's "Te Deum," like all Gregorian music, is written on a stave of four lines, with this cleff:

Tallis's Eighth Tune, taken from Archbishop Parker's Psalter, is written in different cleffs, thus:

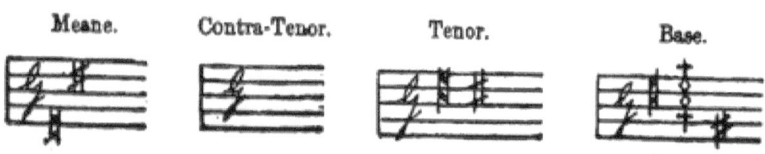

and so on.

A Chronological Table, giving the dates of eminent Composers for the Church, &c., is also annexed, so that it will be easy at a glance to see whose influence was at work at any particular time.

Hampton Road,
    Bristol, 1872.

Chronological List of Composers.

		Born	Died
	Ambrose elected Bishop of Milan ...		374
	Gregory created Pope ...		590
	Guido flourished about ...		1024
	Ockenheim flourished about ...		1450
1	C. Festa ...	born 1498	died 1545
	Dr. Tye ...	,, 1500	,,
	Martin Luther ...	,, 1483	,, 1546
2	C. Goudimel ...	,, 1510	,, 1572
	T. Tallis ...	,, 1520	,, 1585
	Palestrina ...	,, 1524 (?)	,, 1594
	John Dunstable ...	,,	,, 1548
	G. Farnby ...	,,	,, 1598
	Michael Este ...	,, 1550	,, 1600
	J. Playford ...	,,	,,
	T. Morley ...	,, 1560	,, 1602 (?)
	J. Dowland ...	,, 1562	,, 1609
	T. Tomkins ...	,,	,, 1620 (?)
	John Tomkins ...	,,	,, 1638 (?)
	O. Gibbons ...	,, 1583	,, 1625
	Carissimi ...	,, 1585 (?)	,, 1672
	T. Ravenscroft ...	,, 1592	,,
	W. Bird ...	,, 1543	,, 1623
	H. Lawes ...	,, 1600	,, 1662

1 Constanzo Festa wrote the Mass which has been performed at the election of every Pope since his time.

2 Claude Goudimel fell at the massacre of St. Bartholomew; he is supposed by some to have written the tune known as the Old Hundredth. He reckoned Palestrina among his pupils.

Dr. Child	...	...	...	born 1607	...	died 1697
J. B. Lulli	...	...	...	,, 1633	...	,, 1672
R. Creyghton	...	...	...	,, 1639	...	,, 1736
J. Weldon	...	...	...	,, 1670 (?)	...	,, 1736
Dr. Blow	...	...	...	,, 1648	...	,, 1708
Dr. Aldrich	...	...	...	,, 1647	...	,, 1710
P. Humphreys	...	...	...	,, 1647	...	,, 1674
J. Clark	...	...	...	,,	...	,, 1707
Henry Purcell	...	...	...	,, 1658	...	,, 1695
Dr. Croft	...	...	...	,, 1677	...	,, 1727
Handel	...	...	...	,, 1684	...	,, 1759
J. S. Bach	...	...	...	,, 1685	...	,, 1754
J. Travers	...	...	...	,,	...	,, 1758
Dr. Greene	...	...	...	,,	...	,, 1755
Dr. Arne	...	...	...	,, 1710	...	,, 1778
Gluck	...	...	...	,, 1714	...	,, 1787
Dr. Boyce	...	...	...	,, 1710	...	,, 1779
Dr. Nares	...	...	...	,, 1715	...	,, 1783
Dr. Dupuis	...	...	...	,, 1733	...	,, 1796
Haydn	...	...	...	,, 1732	...	,, 1809
Dibdin	...	...	...	,, 1748	...	,, 1814
S. Webbe	...	...	...	,, 1740	...	,, 1817
J. Battishill	...	...	...	,, 1738	...	,, 1801
Mozart	...	...	...	,, 1756	...	,, 1791
C. Wesley	...	...	...	,, 1757	...	,, 1815
S. Wesley	...	...	...	,, 1766	...	,, 1837
T. Attwood	...	...	...	,, 1767	...	,, 1838
Cherubini	...	...	...	,, 1760	...	,, 1842
Dr. Callcott	...	...	...	,, 1766	...	,, 1821
Beethoven	...	...	...	,, 1770	...	,, 1827
Weber	...	...	...	,, 1786	...	,, 1826
Auber	...	...	...	,, 1784	...	,,
Bishop	...	...	...	,, 1787	...	,, 1855
Spohr	...	...	...	,, 1783	...	,, 1859
Rossini	...	...	...	,, 1792	...	,,
Mendelssohn	...	...	...	,, 1809	...	,, 1848

Music in the Western Church.

ALWAYS interesting as it is to trace back institutions and customs to their origin and first foundation—noting here how the primitive idea has lost some of its integrity; and there, how it has drawn to itself seemingly incongruous associations,—the interest is increased tenfold when the direct connection between such and a system of religion is apparent. I say *direct* connection, because every custom for which any degree of universality can be claimed, probably had its birth in a religious superstition of some kind. Man has an essentially religious instinct, and amid the Babel of conflicting opinions concerning the Deity and His relation towards His creatures, one prominent truth, peculiar to none but shared by all, is held by every " people, nation, and language that dwell in the earth "—the truth, namely, of the existence of a God! Though he cannot scientifically demonstrate this existence of a Deity, man nevertheless feels there must be one; nay, more, he feels the Deity within himself! The belief in a Superior Being to ourselves engenders feelings of awe and reverence, and acts of worship are duly prompted. According as our conceptions of the Deity are gross and material, or refined and spiritual, so will the worship offered Him differ in its most important characteristics. Man's ignorance in past times (is he much wiser now?) could not fail to issue in false and degrading notions of the Supreme; from these, and the sequential peculiar devotional acts accompanying them, arose nearly all the customs which have been handed down to us from remote ages. As an illustration, I need only refer to the names of the days of the week, which it is well known are derived from the gods of the ancient mythologies; Easter-cakes, the burning of wax candles in churches, the Mistletoe bough, &c., all had their origin in the religious superstitions of men.

Perhaps the least baneful, and certainly the most beautiful, of the various forms into which the worship of the earlier civilized races came to be moulded, was that of Music. Music was to them a divine art, the gift of Apollo; and "in all nations the first public use of music has been in the celebration of rites and ceremonies." Though it may now be said to have two distinct manifestations, sacred and secular (the distinction between the two being, however, far less well-defined than is commonly supposed; if indeed it be not purely arbitrary), music has remained true to its primal inspiration; for the highest and purest creations, and the most soul-moving and passion-rousing strains, have been either called into being by, or dedicated to, Religion. Epiphanius, writing in the fourth century, said, "It is evident that the first design and use of music was for the praise and glory of God, and to be a part of His worship." This opinion of Epiphanius is the opinion of nearly every modern Church, for music occupies a prominent place in the public devotional services offered to the Deity. It is scarcely necessary to say, however, that the musical portion of these services differs widely from that of primitive times, and even from that of the fourth century. But few of the arts had then seen their highest degree of cultivation; that of music perhaps the least of all. To trace the history of this divine art is not my present purpose. I propose simply to give a popular, yet trustworthy account of its employment in the Western Church; such an account cannot fail to be of more than usual historical interest, while the materials for such are mostly beyond the reach of general readers, being to be found either in expensive books, or else in copies of rare old works only to be met with in our Museums.

That the reader may be placed in as favourable a position as is possible for the complete understanding of the subject, I shall make a few remarks upon the state of music generally, prior to the establishment of the Roman church.

The origin of music, or rather of man's discovery of it, has been the subject of much conjecture; Lucretius taught that "Birds instructed men, who tried to frame their voice and imitate them;" others that the whistling of the wind in the hollow reeds first imparted the notion of music. Franckinus, again, ascribed it to the various sounds produced by the hammers of that very mythical personage, Tubal Cain; Zarlino, to the sound of dropping water; while a recent writer (1) says there is no music in nature, neither melody nor harmony, but that it is the creation of man. "Nature," he says, "gives us sound, and the musician compels it to work his will; the painter transfers to the canvas the forms and tints he sees around him, but the musician does not reproduce any combination of sounds he has ever heard, or could possibly hear, in the natural world." He adds that modern music, which is alone worthy of the name, is but four hundred years old, being the youngest of the arts. To a certain extent this is true, for we can hardly conceive of music as an art, apart from harmony; and this, regarded as a science, is but of recent study. The infancy of every art is lost in obscurity; the lack of means in early times for preserving their acquisitions of knowledge to posterity, renders it hopeless to mark with any certainty the steps by which men approached perfection in the various studies to which they have given themselves. With respect to this particular art of music, its history cannot be

---

(1) Rev. H. R. Haweis.

traced earlier than the history of Egypt : though, as we find upon its ancient monuments representations of musical instruments; and as moreover, vocal must have long preceded instrumental music; we have indisputable testimony to the fact of "sweet sounds" having been made long before the era of Egyptian civilization. Herodotùs tells us that music was regarded by the Egyptians as the gift of inspiration, and its use chiefly restricted to the services held in honour of their deities; but in the absence of any musical records of this period, it is impossible to say what their music was like. From the few instruments which we know to have been in use then, we can only regard it as having been extremely simple.

The earliest mention of music is found in the Pentateuch, and taking into account, as we must, the real time at which this was written, we come to the conclusion that no reliable information is given of earlier date than a thousand years, B.C. In these old Jewish narratives are perhaps to be found the only authentic facts connected with Egyptian music, for it is probable the Israelites acquired their knowledge of the art from their taskmasters. From passages in these early writings we find that poetry was always accompanied by song, and both by instruments. Laban complained that Jacob had not permitted him to send him away "with mirth and with songs, with tabret and with harp." Miriam, after the overthrow of the Egyptians, took a timbrel and sang and danced; indeed, all authorities agree in saying that music and poetry were at first inseparable, and that dancing also had an intimate connection with song. It is probable indeed that music, which was of course first vocal, was intended simply as a vehicle for poetry, either to set it off to greater advantage, or else to aid its committal to memory. No Hebrew music has however come down to us, or at least none that can with certainty be said to be such. Prior to the 15th century the Jews possessed no written music, the melodies being passed on from precentor to precentor, each of whom would doubtless alter the same to suit his own taste. It is just possible however, that the Gregorian Chants came from Jerusalem, (2) but as there is no proof of this, and as moreover, all ancient music had a sameness of character, it would not be safe to affirm it. So completely does history fail us here, that even the meaning of the musical accents appended to the Psalms is uncertain! Josephus tells us 20,000 musicians assisted at the dedication of Solomon's Temple; and one of his annotators adds, "The ancient music of the Hebrews must have been very complete; it embraced a great variety of tunes, as is evident from the number of musical instruments, and by the testimony of Jesus, the son of Sirach, who, in Ecclesiasticus writes, 'The singers sang praises with their voices; with great variety of sounds was there made sweet melody.'" Hebrew, and indeed all oriental music was mostly rhythmical, and would no doubt strike a modern ear as monotonous in the extreme. We find constant references to music in Greek literature; it was the second necessary part of a liberal education, and under it was comprised poetry, dancing, and the drama. All the poets were musicians; one writer affirms that though ancient Greece had many musicians who were not poets, it had no poets who were not also musicians, and who did not compose the music of their own pieces; hence, he says, the superiority of Greek poetry over Latin, as well as that of modern languages. It is difficult for a cold prosaic nature to understand either the intense love of a musician for his art, or the power such an one possesses to express his mental emotion in song, and it is no less difficult for us

---

(2) KIESEWETTER says this is impossible, for "the early Christians' horror at everything connected with the heathen was too great to admit of their using such melodies as were common to the Pagan temples or theatres, and they evinced an equal anxiety to separate themselves from the Jews." He however, is mistaken here, for the rhythm of the early Christian hymns prove them to have been set to the music of the pagan odes.

who live in this utilitarian age to realize the necessity which existed for the early poets to be musicians also. The connection between the two has been recognized by all true poets; when some one remarked to Wordsworth that Tennyson seemed to have a more perfect sense of music than that of any of the new race of poets, the Laureate replied, "Yes, the perfection of harmony lies in the very essence of the poet's nature, and Tennyson gives magnificent proofs that he is endowed with it." Wordsworth's opinion has been fully borne out, for who has not noticed the exceeding beauty of the present Laureate's measures? The tragedies of ancient Greece and Rome were not only sung but accompanied, and for long years instrumental music was not thought of apart from words; this no doubt is to be regretted, as different studies receive their highest cultivation only when separately pursued, and in the present instance there can be no doubt this presumed indissoluble union between song and instrumentation has been greatly to the detriment of the latter, for as the music to the odes of the ancients was evidently little else than recitative (3), no scope was afforded for brilliancy of instrumental execution. Indeed, the music to which the classic epics were sung was not that which would satisfy modern requirements; the art was in its infancy, and but little was known of the wonderful combinations into which sounds can be made to enter. Harmony had not been devised, and their imperfect scale, combined with their ignorance of the use of chromatics, rendered even the melody of the ancients tedious from its sameness.

The style of music to which these Odes, &c., was set, is well shown in Mendelssohn's eight-part chorus, "Œdipus in Colonos," which, though a beautiful composition, would still be unbearably monotonous if heard for one hour; at any rate no conductor appears willing to make the experiment. Many of the Greek dramas

---

(3) Hawkins.

consisted of 1500 verses, and it was not unusual for the leader, (or Coryphœus) to speak either alone or in dialogue with the other players, and thus acquaint the audience with the progress of the events intended to be represented. The chorus sometimes mustered fifty performers, but these were afterwards reduced by law to fifteen. Among the Greeks prizes were offered to the winners in games of physical exercises and intellectual display. History tells us of a prize being offered to the best performer on the flute, about 591 B.C., and in the 96th Olympiad (396 B.C.) another was given to the best player on the trumpet. Pausanias says the Pythic games anciently consisted only of poetical and musical contests, the highest prize being awarded to him who wrote and sang the best hymn in honour of Apollo. It is said that Nero, the inhuman Emperor of Rome, frequently entered the lists, and that, such was the slavish adoration paid him, he was always declared victor. Rome adopted the style of Grecian music, as she did her style of other arts, when that country became subject to her arms (B.C. 146). The flute was the favourite instrument of the time, though it of course lacked the keys and other modern improvements. All instruments were of rude construction, for men had other and more practical matters demanding their attention.

We have thus seen that till now in the pagan world (as it is called) there was but little music apart from the special words to which it was set by the poets themselves; while among the Jews the chants to which the Psalms and other devotional hymns were sung, were orally handed down from one generation to the succeeding—a process singularly liable to errors, if not to innovations. Terpander, who flourished 671 B.C., and who was a poet and musician, is said to have invented a notation and musical characters; but they must have been of little use, and for the large majority of people it must have been as though such things were not. Though music has been called an art in the previous pages, it was not strictly so in these early times, as it received little or no *distinctive* attention; it was, as I have already said, simply regarded as a vehicle for words, *these* being to the performers of the greatest importance. The Hebrews placed their musical characters both above and below the words to be sung, which mode seems to have been general. The Roman church adopted the same plan, though it afterwards improved upon it by drawing a straight line above the words and arranging the notes with a geometrical distance either above or beneath it, according as the voice was to ascend or descend; when instruments were used the player was accompanied in unison. The stave, as we know it, is of much later invention, and as neither bars were used and frequently no cleffs or other distinguishing marks for determining the key in which the music was written—as neither harmony nor the perfect scale were known—it will be easily understood that but little was really known of the principles of music.

We now approach the time from which Music in the Western Church may be said to date, for in the year 62 of our era, Paul was brought to Rome, having appealed unto Cæsar; though there were Christians in that city before Paul's arrival, yet we may safely affirm that had it not been for this great man's undaunted courage, and his inspiring words and presence, the Roman Christian Church would not have assumed those proportions which enabled it successfully to outlive the terrible persecutions it afterwards encountered. No music of this period is preserved, and but little of the hymnody. That music formed part of the service of the primitive church, is however beyond all dispute, for Paul urges the Colossians to teach and admonish one another in Psalms and Hymns, and Spiritual Songs; and later, Clement of Alexandria writes thus, "The singers are holy men, their song is the hymn of the Almighty King; virgins chant, angels glorify, prophets discourse, while music sweetly sounding is heard;" from which we may infer that instruments, (probably stringed) were in use at that time in the Christian church. In his Apostolical constitutions Clement also tells us that after the lessons had been read, the people sang a Hymn or Psalm of David, a presbyter commencing, and the congregation joining in afterwards, as is done now, indeed, in the Papal church. Philo, speaking of the nocturnal assemblies of the Christians, (for those were hard times, and the gatherings were often obliged to be at night and in secret,) says, "After supper their sacred song began. When all were arisen they selected two choirs, one of men and one of women, in order to celebrate some festival, and from each of these a person of majestic form and well skilled in music was chosen to lead the band; they then chanted hymns in honour of God, composed in different measures and modulations, now singing together, and now alternately answering one another." It is here we find the first mention of precentors and antiphonal singing among the primitive Christians, though, as they formed no recognised "Church,"—each congregation managing its own affairs, and doubtless appointing its own order of service, (as it is certain it selected its own Scriptures,)—no one mode was universal; and probably Clement and Philo speak only of the respective congregations known to them. We may be sure that the rhythmical chanting of the Psalms was observed by them, and in all likelihood to the music of the Synagogue, for as Christianity was promulgated by Jews it is probable that the music as well as the liturgy was supplied by them, especially as has been already said, music apart from the special words to which it was set scarcely existed. I say "scarcely," because such was not entirely the case; or if so, the primitive church was the first to adapt other music to their own compositions, for the structure of the few hymns that have come down to us, together with other considerations, lead us to believe they were written in the measure of the "Odes" in order that the same music might be employed for the one as for the other.

About the year 312 Christianity became the established religion of the Roman Empire. Bishops were appointed, and the pagan churches now resounded to the praises of the Christians' God. Increased attention was paid to the proper observance of public worship, and a ritual (no doubt for politic purposes,) was introduced into the church. Eusebius, writing a few years after this event, says, "There was one common consent in chanting forth the praises of God; the performance of the service was exact, the rites of the church decent and majestic, and there was a place appointed for those who sung psalms; youths and virgins, old men and young." By this Eusebius means the choir or leaders of the singing, for in the first centuries the congregations joined heartily in the singing, and were encouraged so to do by their presbyter; no music of this period has come to us. Ambrose, however, now appeared, being made Bishop of Milan, in the year 374; he introduced choral service with antiphonal singing into his church, which had formerly been a pagan sanctuary, and while such had no doubt possessed for those days an elaborate service, for we hear of instruments having been employed there 200 years previously. Ambrose wisely retained the musical character of the old service, so altering it as to suit the reformed worship, adding such new features as to make it a great attraction to outsiders, whom he thus hoped to draw into the church. About this time the Psalmistæ were appointed; their duty was to attend to the musical portion of the service. Hawkins, in his history of music, says that such great confusion and disorder followed from the practice of the whole congregation singing, as necessitated such a selection, and no doubt a choir, for the Psalmistæ were little else, was found to be an essential element of the body ecclesiastic as it is in our days. These men (for they are said to have been an order of the clergy) were duly ordained for the purpose, the fourth council of Carthage prescribing these words to be used at such service:—

" See that thou believe in thy heart what thou singest with thy mouth, and approve in thy works what thou believest in thy heart." We have said that the Roman Empire became Christian early in the fourth century ; by this is meant only that Christianity became the recognized religion of the state. It was in fashion then, and men had to render outward obedience to its dogmas, but the history of the church proves little else was the case. The second generation saw the simple religion of Jesus Christ laden with burdens He never imposed, and darkened by superstitions altogether foreign to His mind. It needs but a moment's reflection to become convinced of the utter absurdity of supposing that the whole Roman Empire became Christians by an edict of the Imperial Court. It was impossible ; and history tells us that Paganism leavened Christianity. The historian Mossheim says, "It is difficult to determine whether the heathens were most Christianized, or Christians most heathenized." As can be easily imagined under such circumstances, the church embraced within its fold men of widely differing opinions, and the various councils were continually being called upon to pronounce against some heresy—or as they too often did—to aid and abet one. But not only were the bishops troubled with these theological matters, but they were frequently required to reform the services, and the manner of conducting them, as these got corrupted. Ambrose seems to have been the first musical reformer of the church, and the music he arranged went for many years by the name of the Cantus Ambrosianus, or the Ambrosian Song. This was sung in unison, and was not accompanied, musical instruments being now banished from the Christian church. It is unlikely that Ambrose composed the four out of the eight Gregorian tones which are usually ascribed to him ; their names indicate their Eastern origin, but he probably arranged them conveniently for his purpose. He also wrote several hymns, setting them to the more appropriate of the heathen melodies which were already to his hand, and which he was too wise completely to ignore. One of these, the "Conditor alme siderum," I now reprint. It is supposed to have been a pagan sacrificial song; for the better forming of comparisons, and noting the growth of psalmody, it should be sung, as it was intended to be sung by its first Christian editor, in unison and unaccompanied.

To us it sounds bald from the want of harmony, but Ambrose himself in one of his sermons, speaking probably of the music of his own cathedral, says, "The effect of the responses of the psalms, the singing of men, women, maidens, and children, is like the breaking of the waves of the sea." Augustine also thus writes of the efforts of Ambrose to reform the church music of his day: "How did I weep through thy hymns and canticles, touched to the quick by the voices of thy sweet-attuned church."

We hear no more of church music till the time of Gregory, A.D. 590; during the years intervening, the four tones or tunes of Ambrose, had become corrupted, probably from the fact of their being but little or no notation in use, the successive precentors consequently failing to preserve them in their original form. Gregory, who was a very good musician, determined to remedy this and also to remodel the service, so in A.D. 590 he re-wrote the Cantus Ambrosianus, which with his own additions, henceforth became known as the Gregorian Song. Ambrose had compiled four tones, which were now called authentic, to these Gregory added four more, called plagal, or appended tones. Of the eight "tones," the first, third, fifth, and seventh, are the Ambrosian, the four others being the Gregorian. The ninth, or Peregrine Tone was not added till some years later.

Gregory wrote out an order of service, comprising psalms, responses, &c., and his Antiphonarium, subsequently revised and enlarged, is used to this day in the Roman Catholic church. It was this pope who sent Augustine to Britain, who naturally brought with him the music as well as the teaching of his church. What our music was before this period it is difficult to say ; of a wild plaintive character no doubt, and the instruments must have been very rude. Temple worship there was none, as most of the religious rites of the ancient Britons were performed in the open air.

Augustine remedied this, and converted our great-forefathers to his religion and its accessories. The Gregorian music was simple, and being sung in unison it must have sounded to the wondering natives very grand and beautiful compared with their own wild songs. It certainly took deep root in England, and to it as the source, is credited all our ecclesiastical music. Rome took the lead in musical reform ; not only here, but into Germany was this new song introduced, displacing all other music, and so affecting the very springs of native genius as to have found its way at length into the work of the great masters, notably Handel and Mendelssohn. It is true that Hawkins tells us the endeavours to establish the Gregorian song in Britain were so ill-received by the clergy that it occasioned the slaughter of 1200 of them at once, but this statement must be received with caution. Hawkins was a musician, and no theologian ; had he been the latter, he would have discovered that the opposition of the people was directed, not against the *music*, but against the *practices* of the Roman church, which was bent upon abolishing the native feasts and substituting its own in their place.

I give here the first Gregorian tone ; nearly all the tones

have several endings. This example is the first tone, third ending. It should be sung as it probably was at its first institution, one voice commencing the first verse, and the people, divided into two choirs, singing the remainder of the psalm antiphonally.

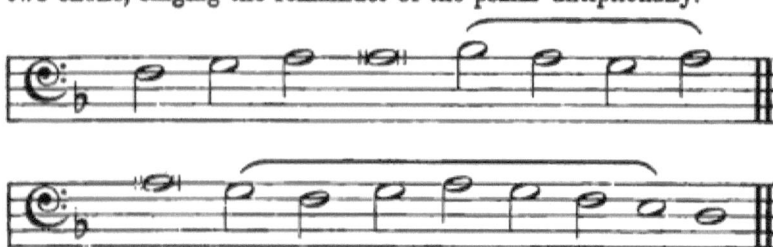

The object of one voice leading off in this way would seem to be that of informing the congregation what music was about to be sung to the psalm. In those days instruments were not employed in public worship, so that the music could not be played over as it is in modern churches. I need hardly add that this custom is still retained in the Roman Catholic church, and to a certain extent in the Anglican church also. It is a very ancient custom, and can be traced back to David's time, if not earlier, for many of the Psalms were written for the purpose of being sung by two choirs, one answering the other. The next example is one of the plagal tunes, one of Gregory's own. It is a stirring melody, and well adapted to the words of the 150th Psalm.

Without altogether condemning these "tones," we cannot fail to notice that their unisonity is very tedious, and that a certain monotonousness pervades them. I certainly cannot give them that unqualified praise which the Anglican party so lavishly bestows on them. It is very doubtful whether their revival of late years has not been entirely due to the fact of their having been instituted by

Gregory, who was a decided ritualist; and also perhaps to this other fact, that they are the oldest-known specimens of church music. Though it is remembered that to this day the Papal church uses the Gregorian song, and as a rule sing it in unison, the organ occasionally filling in harmonies; and while it is possible that the choirs occasionally lack that reverence which should always be observed when singing the praises of God; and though Mendelssohn tacitly admitted a sort of beauty in the tones by incorporating them into his works, using them as "subjects," we yet must acknowledge he had good grounds for writing as he did from Rome : " It shocks me to hear the most solemn and beautiful words chanted along to such unmeaning hurdy-gurdy sounds." Luther spoke even more strongly about them, not hesitating to liken them to a "dismal ass's bray!" It was in the fifth century the Te Deum was composed. Tradition says it gushed forth from the lips of Ambrose while he was baptising Augustine in Milan Cathedral, or that they both sang it then, taking alternate verses. This of course is but tradition. Dr. Rimbault is of the opinion it was composed by Nicettus, Bishop of Triers, about 500.

The following is a hymn composed in honour of John the Baptist. The music is to be referred to a period not later than the fifth century. It will afford us the opportunity of noticing the peculiar structure of the early metrical music, and it is interesting also from its having suggested to Guido, some five hundred years later, the Sol-Fa notation.

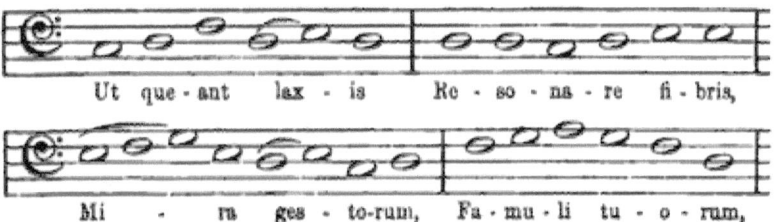

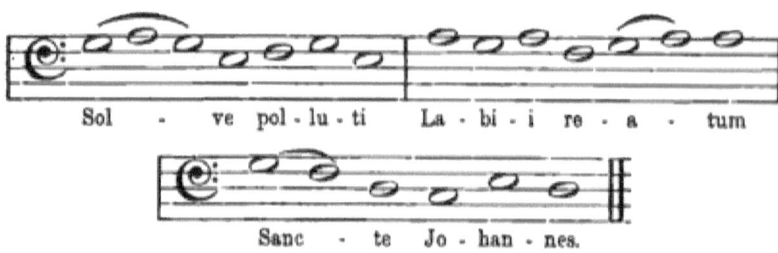

For long years no improvement was made in the Gregorian music, and but comparatively little new music that we know of was written; by slow degrees the notation was improved, this being at first but a very poor attempt at writing music. Mr. Hullah says that hundreds of volumes exist without a single sharp or flat, the singers having rules for the alteration of notes during the performance; he says also that till the beginning of the seventh century there were no bars; these latter have only come into general use in modern times. The staff of one line had gradually increased to ten lines by the eighth century, on which crooks and strokes (or neumas, as they were called,) were placed; there was no universally recognized notation however, each composer adopting that which seemed to him best. Hucbald tells of a composition of the tenth century in which the words were printed in spaces between lines, each space meaning a particular tone or interval, and each syllable placed in the space to which the tune would assign it. The seventh century saw the introduction of organs. While mention is made of organs in writings previous to this date, it is tolerably certain they bore little resemblance to the instruments now brought forward. (4)

---

(4) The date of the invention of organs is a vexed question; scarcely any two writers agree on the matter. One authority states Marinus Samutus, (surnamed Torcellus,) introduced wind organs into the church about A. D. 1290. Thomas Aquinas in 1250, wrote "Our church does not use musical instruments, as harps and psalteries to praise God withal, that she may not seem to Judaize." Does he mean the church used *no* instruments?

Pope Vitalianus has the credit of first erecting organs in churches in the year 660, and as if to show how averse human nature is to change, Hawkins has an amusing anecdote to the effect that the enemies of church music objected very strongly, as the Scotch Presbyterians do now, to the employment of organs in public worship, going so far as to insinuate it was in the year 666 organs were first used in churches, inferring from this the unlawfulness of the innovation, that number corresponding with the number of the beast in the Apocalypse.

By the middle of the ninth century organs were common all over Europe, and the tenth century saw them established in England. The year 886 saw a musical professorship founded by king Alfred, at Oxford.

But a greater change than even the introduction of organs had been made before this latter date—I refer to harmony. All church music had hitherto been sung in unison, and, where accompanied, with the instruments also in unison. As the study of music received more general attention, men were no longer satisfied with such a meagre display, and at last Hucbald, a Flemish monk, made an attempt to introduce harmony into the church services by adding to the air (or principalis) an accompaniment, usually of progressive fourths and fifths. But it must not be inferred this was the first use of harmony. Isidore, of Seville, in his "Sententiæ de Musica," mentions two kinds of harmony: symphony, and diaphony, the former being a combination of consonant, and the latter a combination of dissonant intervals. As this was a little subsequent to the first barbarian invasion of the south of Europe, Isidore thinks the notion of harmony came from the north, and he mentions the fact of ancient British and Russian instruments being made with two or three strings which must have been sounded *together*. But harmony is really very much older than this, for many ancient sculptures are found with illustrations of stringed instruments, which were evidently played with both hands. From the biblical account of the musicians dedicated to the service of Solomon's temple, we may also gather that different notes were played by different instruments at the same time. It may, however, be doubted whether the *voices* sung in harmony ; as no written music of this period has come down to us, it is impossible to speak with any certainty concerning it. The singing of another part now above and now below a melody is nevertheless of very ancient date, and the rules for so doing have been handed down verbally from one generation to another from "olden times," till now that written music and the giving of the melody to the highest voice has done away with the necessity of such, these links connecting us with the past have almost disappeared. In our own country, Bede mentions descant as having been practised in his day. Ancient authorities tell us it was regarded with suspicion by the clergy before Hucbald's time, and that while it did very well so to treat secular music, descant was not to be allowed to enter the church door. It was not possible, however, to keep descant out, and by degrees, gradual no doubt, it soon became a recognised institution. At first this accompaniment was as easy as the air itself. It was called organum or descantus, and originally was an extempore invention of the singer; but as it was left with the performers to sing just what, and how they liked, they, in order to shew off their skill, soon introduced a highly florid style, which sometimes descended into the burlesque. Morley says, "Descant is generally taken for singing a part extempore on a playne-song, so that when a man talked of a descanter, it must be one that can extempore sing a part upon a playne-song;" and therefore as the stave was seldom used for more than the melody before the time of Guido, the descant was, as Mr. Hullah says, lost as soon as uttered. I give two examples taken from Hucbald's "Enchiriadis ;" the descant, or harmony as he would call it, is of course rough in the extreme, and if sung with as much force as the principal or air, would be unbearable. The principal, however, was sustained by the whole congregation, a few voices only singing the descant. The examples must be sung thus so as to give as correct an idea as possible of these first attempts at harmonising the church service. The first is for two parts only; the air and the descant upon it.

The second example is a more ambitious attempt, being written for three parts, one above and one below the principal.

The Gregorian music as used at present in the Roman Catholic church, is printed in square notes on a stave of four lines. Though it goes by his name, this mode of printing music was not an invention of Gregory's, for the square notes were not invented till 600 years—nor was the stave of four lines used for the playne-song of the church till 800 years—later. Cantus fermus or "plain song"

was the name given to the air when descant came to be practised, and it naturally fell to what in after years was called the tenor voice, (from the Latin word teneo, I hold,) because this part contained, or held the melody. Cantus means a song, and dis-cantus or descant is a song against another song. When some years later it came to be *written*, it was called contra punctum or counter-point, because as music was then written in points, the added parts of course consisted of points set against other points. It is necessary to remember that meantime the world had not oeen without so-called secular music; dancing, originally a religious exercise, soon came to be a pleasant pastime, and as the dancers of old usually accompanied themselves, so dance music came to be a distinctive branch of the science, and to receive special attention.

As civilization increased, the separation of the twin sister arts—music and poetry—became confirmed, and as poets arose who never wrote music for their compositions, so also did musicians arise whose sole aim it was to sing to their own melodies the verses of others. This was inevitable so soon as something better than mere recitative was found, for music then demanded its followers' entire devotion; it may be said with equal truth of musicians, as of poets, that they are not made but born. Secular melody—for counterpoint was scarcely employed for aught else but church music till the 13th century—thus received great attention, and soon grew into graceful form; whereas melody in the church having been forbidden all play since the times of Ambrose and Gregory, (who succeeded too well in fast stereotyping their own ideas upon this matter,) was now, in the tenth century, as plain and as monotonous as it had been five hundred years before. The difference was of course strongly marked, and hence, no doubt, the origin of that church style which seems so engraven upon all true church music. The introduction of descant did not mend matters, for while florid parts were added to the air or plain song, *this* remained as uninteresting as before. Isidore, whom I have already quoted, said the primitive Christians sang with so small a variation of the voice that it differed little from reading, and he seems to have regarded this style as the best pattern the church could follow. Gregory, whose influence in church music we have seen to have been very great, evidently held similar views, in which perhaps he was strengthened by a desire to make the music of the church as different as possible from the secular music; the Gregorian song is certainly about as plain as music well can be, and but seldom do you meet with a greater interval than a third, more usually the notes proceeding by tones simply. The early attempts at descant were, as we have seen, but little more than a progression of common chords, but the rapid cultivation of melody outside the church could not but affect at least its counterpoint, and very soon we find this not only more tuneful and lively, but popular songs themselves written as descant upon the church song. These ornamental parts were always sung by male voices. There is every reason to suppose that as in the Papal chapel, so in all churches, the choirs were composed of men. Women were then excluded from a higher education, and indeed, in these early times, education was almost exclusively confined to the clergy. Nearly every post of emolument and honour was held by them; few else could either read or write. The study of music was regarded in Rome as a sure and easy road to church preferment, and the clergy jealously guarded their own interests; hence this order was alone able to supply materials for choirs. (5) The absence of female voices of course precluded the setting of high music, though by the use of the falsetto voice, and by the employment (in later years) of boys, a considerable altitude was attained.

---

(5) And indeed, these only were *allowed* to be "professed church singers;" for such is Neander's interpretation of the oft-quoted decree of the council of Laodicea.

The stave was still in a very unsatisfactory state, each school having its own arrangements and notation; the scale as made and used by Ambrose and Gregory, with reference to a supposed mathematical requirement, was found not to answer the demand made upon it, and musical *science* was now in need of a reformer. In the year 1020, the right man appeared in the person of Guido, a monk of Arezzo in Tuscany. He appears to have made the science of music his study, and he was fortunately able to bring his discoveries into practical use. The stave was reduced by him to four lines, and this number is still employed for Gregorian music. Guido is further credited with noticing that in the hymn to John the Baptist, which has been already referred to, each phrase or line of the hymn commenced on the note immediately above the first note of the preceding phrase; this suggested to him a plan for teaching others to sing. Mr. Hullah says no mention is made by Guido in his writings of the Sol-fa syllables; he however used this air, and it is said the ease with which he taught the choristers to sing from notes astonished all who heard them. It had hitherto taken years to master the rudiments of singing, but now with the improved scale, sight-singing was made easy. Guido's scale however was not perfect; it consisted but of six notes, ut, re, mi, fa, sol, la; but imperfect as it was, this hexachord or scale of six sounds, was only abandoned in this century. The si or te is quite a modern addition. Guido is said to have been the first who introduced the use of points with which to write music; the crook and other marks then in use, being but awkward contrivances. He also employed the space between the lines as well as the lines themselves for placing these points upon. The present notation was not perfected till the middle of the 14th century.

These improvements, notably the re-arranging of the scale, had a great effect upon the progress of musical art, for while the melody was still little better than chanting, the harmonics built upon it became more and more graceful, and for the sake of this counterpoint schools were established, which in after years produced those musical geniuses who gave to the Western Church that wealth of song and harmony which has been its glory ever since. But this was a work of time ; meanwhile several agencies were at work which had a decidedly bad effect upon congregational singing, if indeed they were not brought into being for the express purpose of silencing the great body of worshippers. The Latin language, as a dialect, had naturally suffered from the northern invasions, and in the more distant west, where the Gothic element of course prevailed, Latin was a dead language, save to the learned few. When the first attempts were made to plant Christianity on foreign soils, Roman missionaries had, I presume, to address the conquered races in their respective languages, and no doubt the liturgies they imposed were translated into the common dialect, else indeed, how could the people understand or take an interest in the proceedings? In the 11th century, Gregory VII. directed that henceforth the church service should no longer be rendered in the vernacular, giving as the reason, that "general and loud singing would corrupt science." Congregational singing was thus virtually forbidden, and the musical portion of the service being relegated to the choirs, complicated music was adopted, so that with the priest and choir dividing the service between them, nothing was left for the people to do but sit and listen; not a very wise proceeding, as we shall presently see, for if men have the gift of song, (and they undoubtedly have,) and are forbidden to exercise it in one place, it is only natural to suppose they will find some place in which they can give it vent.

About A.D. 1330 John de Muris introduced the time table ; in one of his manuscripts he seems to refer its invention to Franco, who lived about 1083, (some fifty years after Guido, and who employed certain characters to denote the duration of sounds,) but there is no doubt De Muris greatly improved it, and he probably was the first to urge its adoption for church music. Before his time there seems to have been no marks employed, and musicians were left to their own choice in determining what length each sound should be, though they were guided doubtless by a certain common usage. (6) The musical characters or notes in use at this time were chiefly square.

Attention had lately been paid to harmony outside the church, and towards the close of the 13th century we find Adam de la Hale, (b. 1240,) writing songs in three parts; to him is ascribed the first comic opera.

The terms employed at present to denote these various parts are corruptions of the Latin names given them at this period. First there was the tenor, which still, and for long years after, held the tune or melody; next came the contra-tenor, or counter-tenor, so called because it frequently opposed the tenor in contrary motion, sometimes above the melody and now crossing and going below it. The bassus or base, (our bass,) was then added; this was, as its name denotes, the lowest part of all. Above was placed the altus or high part, (our alto,) and over that again, though not till later, when the voices of boys or women were employed, came the triplum (our treble,) it being the third part above the tenor. A fourth and even a fifth part were occasionally added, called respectively quadruplum and quintuplum, but so seldom as not to merit further mention here. The following is a tune written in three parts, in square black notes on a stave of five lines with bars at the end of short phrases, which has come down to us from the 12th century.

---

(6) Mr. Hullah says, Franco, of Cologne, (Hawkins calls him Franco, of Liège,) about whose "date" there is some dispute, but who probably lived about the middle of the 12th century, wrote the first treatise on the Cantus Mensurabilis. Mr. H. adds that notes now first appear to have been used, and sharps and flats came into being.

Chaucer and others of our early poets, frequently speak of the pleasure they derived from the music of their time, but scarcely an example has come down to us. It was the custom in early times for armies to sing heroic songs when advancing to meet an enemy, and Burney, in his history of music, gives one such written in praise of Roland, which was sung at the battle of Hastings. It is a French song and is interesting as an illustration of the music of the period. It was apparently a favourite song of the French army, for they sang it again at the battle of Poictiers. Burney says, the only *English*

song of so early a date as 1400, that came to his knowledge, was one written after the victory of Agincourt in 1415; this however, was probably handed down by tradition, for Hawkins tells us "the most ancient English song with musical notes, perhaps anywhere extant, is 'Summer is a coming in,'" and this probably dates from the middle of the 16th century.

Counterpoint was thoroughly established now, and history speaks of Guillaume Defay as a well-known master and teacher of that art: he composed for four voices. The first example of regular four-part music is a mass written on the occasion of the coronation of Charles V. of France (1360). The introduction of motetts and masses dates from the close of the 14th century, while about the middle of the 15th the fugue was founded by Johannes Ockenheim. Music participated in the general revival of the arts, and as if to make up for long years of neglect, musical compositions were produced in profusion.

The art of printing music in letter-press or on metal type, which Hawkins says was invented in Italy in 1515 or 1516, of course greatly facilitated the cultivation of the art, and as the demand increased, so also did the supply increase. Orlandus Lassus is said to have written two thousand compositions, comprising hymns, psalms, and litanies, as well as many motetts for from four to eight parts. Schlüter credits this musician with having first introduced the use of chromatics, and the employment of the terms Adagio, Allegro, &c.; the time table likewise was further improved by him. Generally speaking, these compositions were little suited for the purpose for which they were intended, and but few have come down to our day. The melody or plain church song was, we can well believe, dull and prosaic—in fit agreement with the traditions of the church, but the descant was such as at length to call down upon it the severest censure. I remarked just now that popular songs were sometimes used for this purpose. Ecclesiastical musicians had frequently taken such and engrafted them upon music set to sacred words. The evil however did not end here: as though the airs themselves were not sufficient, the *words* of these secular songs were occasionally sung as well. Many manuscripts shew that while one part was singing sacred words, the others might be singing some amorous strains or jesting rhymes. Then, too, musical expression was a thing not studied; when writing music for some psalm or service, the first ideas which entered the composer's head were jotted down, quite irrespective of whether words and music suited each other; that the meaning of the words should be brought out and expressed as far as possible in the music, seems never to have been thought of; a fault which English composers exhibited in a marked degree some years later. Such profanity as I have described could not be tolerated for long, and two Councils pronounced against it. The Council of Trent in 1562, condemned the abuses which had crept into the music of the church, and censured those who had thus mixed up with it lascivious songs, while the Council of Bâle decreed that in future no mass or motett of which profane words formed a part, should be performed; it also banished from the church all music built on secular themes—apparently desirous of returning once more to the "old church style;" so distinct was the church from the secular style, (the "church" having always remained the same,) that this resolution virtually excluded all music save the Gregorian. It was soon felt however that this measure was too sweeping, so Palestrina, to whom a recent writer has said modern melody owes its existence, was applied to, and he fortunately more than exceeded the anticipations of those who wished to preserve for the church the best which music could offer. Palestrina in response to their appeal, wrote three masses, dedicating them to a pope who had befriended him in past years. The music of this age is to our modern ears heavy and rather wearisome; the employment solely of male voices was of course a great hindrance to the free out-come of musical ideas, for music had to be written low, in order that it might be sung with ease. A friend of mine who has carefully studied the history of male voice singing with special reference to the counter-tenor, believes that Palestrina's music, as originally written, never rose above C in the third space of the treble cleff. From that time down to the present Rome has not been without great musicians, who have willingly laid their gifts at her feet. Of the immortal masses of Mozart, Haydn, and Beethoven, who shall speak? They speak for themselves as we can not, and to the end of time these free-will offerings will ever tell of a devotion pure and true.

Though the Church may not claim for herself all the best and greatest musical compositions, it may at least be said that all have been written under the religious inspirations which it is her duty to kindle.

Dissent will now claim our attention, and most gladly do we bestow it; for while we love the anthem and the mass, we love the congregational hymn tune still more, and it is tolerably certain that had not Luther been a musician as well as a protestor against the glaring abuses of the Papal system, our psalmody would now be little better than the plain song of the middle ages, which with the more pretentious anthem, was about this time unquestionably monopolized by the choir. In 1517 Luther nailed his theses to the church door of Wittenburg. He was anxious to bring the people to see as he did upon theological matters; free himself from the trammels of a religion which placed a priest between the soul and its spirit-father, he longed to make known the glorious liberty in which he stood; but what was he, a poor monk, to do against the array Rome was able to bring against him? The richer class would not hear him, and the ignorant superstition of the poor made them willing slaves to those who traded upon their fears. But Luther had a soul for music, and sitting one day in his study, depressed and worn, the voice of a street singer caught his ear; the minstrel was singing a hymn composed by one of Luther's early friends, and it suggested to him the idea of endeavouring to spread his own views by such means. He soon collected some hymns breathing his own spirit—writing several himself; and taking for his models, *not* the liturgical choir song of the Roman church, but the sacred songs of the Bohemian and Moravian brethren, he selected and composed suitable melodies for them. These melodies are grand in the extreme, and the Lutheran church was happy in thus having for her founder one who was able to establish a pure faith and a noble congregational psalmody. Following Luther there came other poets and musicians, so that in the year 1851, Germany could boast of 80,000 hymns, and a large number of Chorales or tunes.

What Ambrose was to the Latin, Luther is said to have been to the German church song; he ranked music next in importance to theology, and did his best to ensure "that the words were worthily expressed, not babbled nor drawled." He was particular, too, that the whole body of the people should join devoutly in the singing. So well did he succeed in imparting his own enthusiasm to the crowds who flocked to hear him; so soul-stirring were the melodies he offered to the people, and so powerfully did these appeal to their strong latent power of song, that the Germans actually *sang* themselves into the reformed doctrines. Luther's enemies said he had done them more harm by his songs than by his sermons, and that his psalmody, together with the translation of the Bible into the vernacular, was the chief cause of the speedy spread of the Protestant faith. The very ignorance of the common people, while it made them an easy prey to an unscrupulous priesthood, served Luther in good turn, for while admitting that "Music hath power to charm," we must also insist that this power is in *inverse ratio* to the civilization of a race. In an uncultivated age men give way to their natural feelings; before the judgment is formed, or ever discrimination has been learnt, then has music the greatest influence over the feelings and sentiments. This may be said of all the arts. It is the early days of a nation that are its most poetical ones; poetry and music then have freeër play, and produce more powerful effects. It is not an elaborate classical performance that will rouse the feelings of a crowd, but a few simple words set to a popular and simple air.

"The first Lutheran hymn book appeared at Wittenburgh in 1524, and was called 'An attempt at an arrangement of a German mass.'" It contained several songs of Luther's own writing, and the whole were arranged for four-part singing, the melody being in the tenor, as was customary. One celebrated chorale is Luther's "Ein feste burg ist unser Gott." It is his version of the 46th psalm, and is said to have been composed by him while hiding in the castle of Coburg, during the sitting of the Diet of Augsburg. In modern Tune books it is known by the name of a German town—

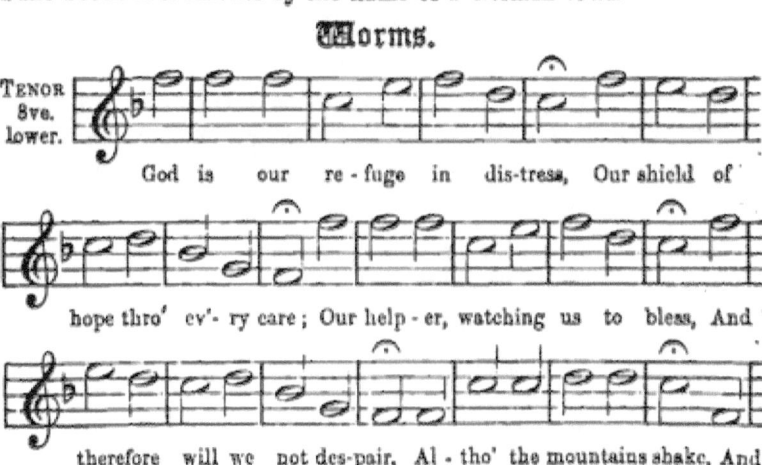

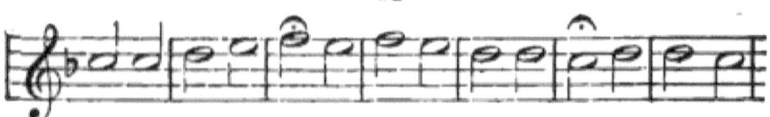
hills their p'ace forsake, And wa-ters o'er them break, Yet still will

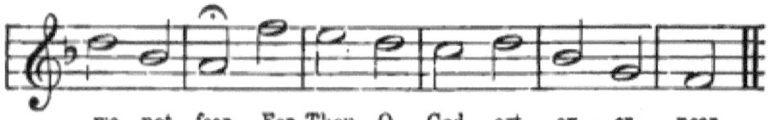
we not fear, For Thou O God, art ev-er near.

It is truly a magnificent melody, and is deservedly worthy of being sung (as it is) on every great national ecclesiastical occasion. Several of these chorales have been adopted by English compilers of Tune-books, and they usually rank first in order of merit in such collections. Dr. Rimbault says, "Though more than three centuries have passed away, the specimens left by Luther have been rarely equalled, and never surpassed."

A little later, Calvin appeared; he seems to have had little love for music, but finding it almost impossible to get on without it, he prudently resolved to have a psalter for *his* churches; so having persuaded Theodore Beza to complete a metrical version of the Psalms, which had been left in an unfinished condition by Marôt, he employed Franc to compose melodies for it. (7) This was published about 1561, and a copy is to be seen in the library of St. Paul's Cathedral. Franc composed for the 134th psalm of this version, the air now known as the Old Hundredth, as well as other melodies which are still popular favourites. While this movement was going on in Germany, a similar one was taking place in our own country. The Reformation seems to have brought with it a universal love of psalm-singing. Myles Coverdale published the first Tune-book in England, about 1538; it was entitled "Goostly Psalms, and Spiritual Songs," and contained metrical versions of

---

(7) The first editions of the French Psalter "noted" were not harmonized.

fifteen psalms and of twenty-six selections from other parts of the Bible. In it are several of the German Chorales, necessity compelling Coverdale, in the absence of an English Choral writer, to make use of the Lutheran tunes. The book gave offence to the capricious monarch, Henry VIII., who condemned it, with other works, to be publicly burnt the year following. But this foolish act was of no avail; the English nation took to psalm singing even as the Germans had done. Bishop Jewel wrote in 1560, "You may now sometimes see at Paul's cross, after the service, 6000 persons, old and young, of both sexes, all singing together and praising God." He adds, "this sadly annoys the mass-priests and the devil, for they perceive that by these means the sacred discourses sink more deeply into the minds of men, and that their kingdom is weakened and shaken at almost every note." Since that time each year has seen fresh accessions to our church psalmody. In September of the year 1547, the Litany translated into English was sung at St. Paul's, and the year following it was ordered to be generally used. 1550 saw the whole Cathedral service in English set to music by John Marbeck, organist of Windsor. The Te Deum and Canticles are set to Gregorian music (in square notes on a stave of four lines); the music will, no doubt, be considered dull and monotonous, but as a faithful specimen of the church song of the time, I here give it. Every syllable has its note in accordance with the suggestion of Cranmer. (8)

We praise Thee O God, We know-ledge Thee to be the Lord.

(8) Cranmer, in his report to Henry VIII. upon the question of translating the Liturgy into English, suggested "the song there-unto should not be full of notes, but as near as may be for every syllable a note, so that it may be sung distinctly and devoutly."

Mary's accession to the throne, in 1553, of course put a stop to the spread of psalmody among the people; her reign however, was happily short, and in the second year of her successor, (1559) a Bill for the uniformity of common prayer was passed. It allowed the Rubric to be either said or sung, and ordained that in "quires" and places where they sing, the Anthem should follow at a certain part of the service. (9) The 16th century was a memorable one for the English church. Our native church music may be said to date from this period. It was the era of Tallis, Dowland, Morley, Daye, Sternhold, Hopkins, Tye, Archbishop Parker, and others. Daye published a Tune-book in 1563; some of the tunes are by English composers, and they are all harmonized by the best musicians of the time. One of these tunes, in two parts only,—the tenor, and the medius as descant—is here given. I have already defined descant as a song set against another song, and I stated that sometimes this added part crossed the melody. This tune is a good example of such crossing; the medius or descant, though it commences on the third above the melody, yet immediately crosses it, and does not again rise above it till the end of the second strain; the beginning of the third strain sees it again below, and so on.

---

(9) Elizabeth enjoined her clergy "that there be a modest and distinct song, so used in all the common prayers of the church, that the same may be plainly understood, as if it were without singing; and in the beginning or end of common prayer, there be sung a hymn in the best melody and music that may conveniently be devised, having respect that the sentiment of the hymn may be perceived and understood." Burney says, "In the latter end of the 15th and the whole of the 16th century, almost every movement of a motett or mass, was built upon some chant or tune, so that while the congregation sang the plain-song, the choristers and choir-men performed the new and more difficult melodies which had been super-added to it."

Tallis composed largely for the English church service, and though to Marbeck belongs the honour of first adjusting the *melody* of the Cathedral service to the English Litany, it was Tallis who first *harmonized* it; his harmony consists chiefly of common chords, and the whole is founded on the Gregorian song, of which Tallis was certainly a great admirer; wanting in brilliancy of style, the effect is nevertheless grand and solemn.

Dr. Tye was also a Church composer, and is noted for his metrical version of the first fourteen chapters of the Book of Acts, which he set to elaborate music—fugues, canons, &c.!

The Gregorian chants were now frequently harmonized, the melody still remaining in the tenor. From complaints of the Puritans a few years later, we must suppose it was still the custom to sing them antiphonally. One such chant was the following; the priest led off the first verse by himself, and the choir, divided in two parts, then joined in—a few voices singing the descant.

Towards the close of the 16th century an attempt was made to place the melody in the treble, but without success.

Lucas Ossiander, in the preface to a Psalter he published in 1586 having the tunes thus arranged, says, "I know very well that composers are in the habit of assigning the chorale (that is the melody) to the tenor. But if this be done, the chorale cannot be distinguished from one of the other parts; the common people cannot tell what psalm it is, nor join in the singing. For this reason I have placed the chorale in the treble, so that it shall be recognised distinctly, and every lay member can sing too."

Leo Hassler, a celebrated organist of that period, expressed the same opinion. It is evident from the above quotation, that the choirs must have consisted of an equal number of voices to each part, because one part could not be distinguished from another. It is also evident that the clerical element still predominated in choirs. In England, this re-arrangement of the parts was not effected till after the Restoration. Dr. Rimbault thinks that "on account of the increase of choirs the people ceased to join in the singing, and that to accommodate the voices of boys who were now employed to sing the plain-song, the melody was given to the treble." It is probable, however, that the introduction of a dramatic style had a great deal to do with the silencing of the congregation.

Archbishop Parker published a Psalter about 1565, which contained nine tunes by Tallis; these are founded on the Gregorian tones, and are prefaced by these lines:—

> The first is meeke; devout to see,
> The second sad: in majesty.
> The third doth rage, and roughly brayth,
> The fourth doth fawne, and flattry playth,
> The fyth delighth, and laugheth the more,
> The sixt bewayleth, it weepeth full sore,
> The seventh tredeth stoute, in froward race,
> The eyghte goeth milde, in modest pace.

Then follow instructions as to the manner of singing them; "the tenor of these partes be for the people when they will syng alone, the other partes for greater queers, or to such as will syng or play privately." The music for each part is printed separately; that for the Meane and the Contra-tenor on one page, and that for the Tenor and the Base on the other. The tune which Tallis composed for the 97th psalm, "The one" that "goeth milde, in modest pace," is given below. It is the original of our Evening Hymn; the air is in the tenor, and the whole tune was evidently intended as a canon.

In 1583 a Tune-book was published with this extraordinary title, "Seven Sobs of a Sorrowful Soul for Sinne comprehending those seven psalms of the princelie prophet David commonly called Pœnitentiall reduced into meter by William Hunnis whereunto are also annexed his handful of honisuckles."

The close of this century saw the Congregational Hymn Tune universally adopted. Organs, which I am inclined to think had at first been pretty much confined to conventual establishments, were now to be found in most places of worship, and were used, in conjunction with choirs, to tone down by harmony the somewhat harsh sound of a melody sung in unison by a large body of people.

1592 was the natal year of Ravenscroft. At the age of fourteen he took his degree of Bachelor of Music, and in 1621 he brought out his Psalter, which was decidedly the best that had yet appeared. It was called "The Whole Book of Psalmes with the Hymnes Evangelicall and Songs Spirituall composed into 4 parts by sundry authors to such severall tunes as have beene and are usually sung in England, Scotland, Wales, Germany, Italy, France, and the Netherlands; never as yet before in one Volume published." The book opens with an address to "Harmonical Brethren," and in it Ravenscroft gives a brief sketch of the history of music. Like Parker's Psalter, the music for the various parts was printed separately; that for the Cantus and the Tenor was on one page, that for the Medius and Bassus on the other. The notes of this and other Psalters of the time are lozenge-shaped, and but little attention is paid to barring. The clefs in these old books are very puzzling, and require much skill in decyphering; leger lines were evidently a bugbear to musicians, and recourse was had to various clefs, in order to avoid them. Sometimes, each of the four parts of a tune is written in a different clef. The first tune I have selected from this celebrated Psalter is that set to the 104th Psalm in metre; the music is by Ravenscroft himself.

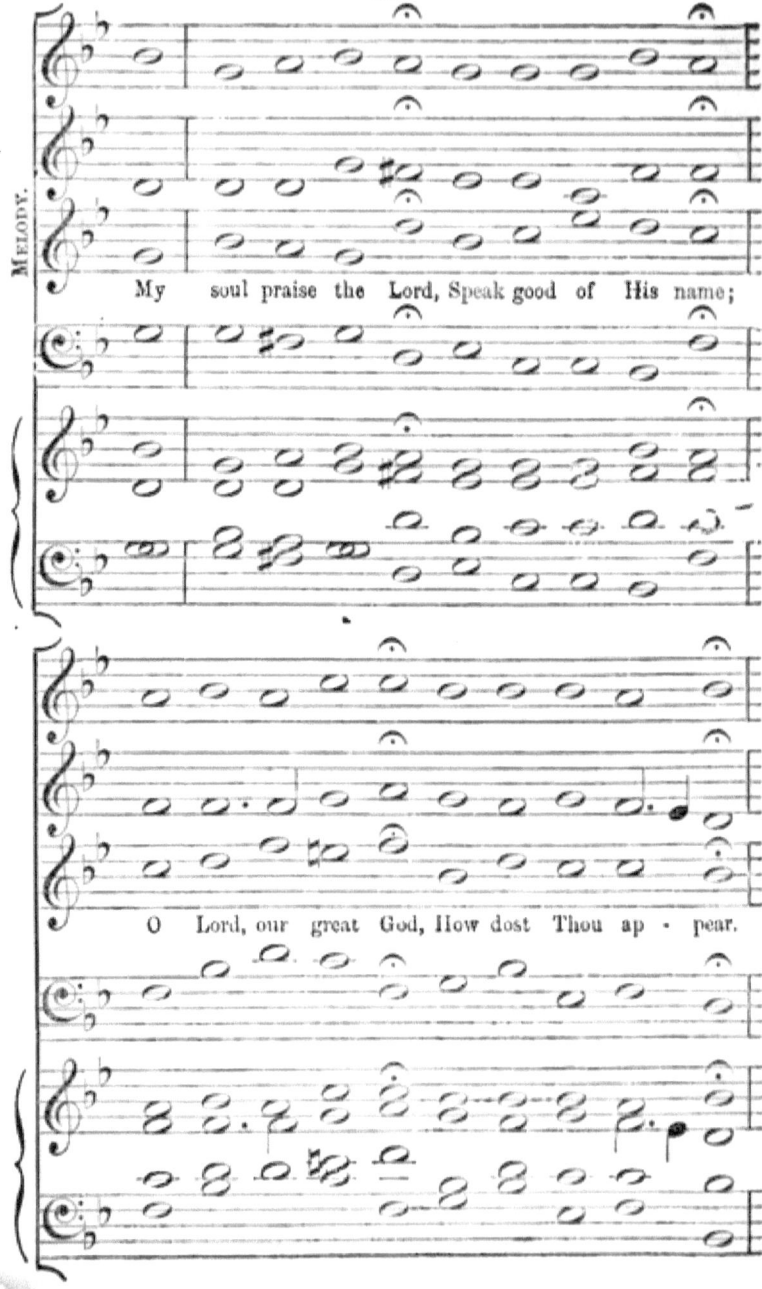

I have said that Franc, Calvin's assistant, composed the tune now known as the Old Hundredth. Calvin cared little for music and nothing for harmony, consequently in the Tune-books of the early Calvinistic churches we seldom get anything but the air. Usually a metrical version of the Psalms " noted " throughout is bound up with the Bible. The next example is this tune of Franc's, harmonized by Dowland, as it appears in Ravenscroft's Psalter. In arranging words to melodies, particular care was always taken that each syllable should be sung to one note ; the harmonies, however, were frequently so intricate and so difficult as to compel us to regard the singers of those times with great respect, for nothing but a good knowledge of music could have rendered it possible for them to sing some of the parts set as descant. The harmonies built upon the melody of the Old Hundredth are by no means easy to sing, and the arbitrary syncopations make them still more difficult.

The next tune from this work which I shall give is Ravenscroft's edition of Tallis's Eighth Tune in Parker's Psalter. It was originally written for a hymn of sixteen lines, four syllables in each line. Ravenscroft called it "a Psalm before Morning Prayer," and shortened it one half, setting it to an ordinary long-metre hymn. Several of the old tunes have been so altered (sometimes we admit judiciously) that the composers would have some difficulty in recognising them as their own. The melody is very fine, and as hymns of the peculiar-metre for which it was originally composed are seldom met with, we must not be too severe in this instance upon its various editors.

By comparing this tune with its original, (see page 42) it will be seen that Ravenscroft has wisely omitted the repetitions, (which only weakened the tune) and this, too, without spoiling the canon. In this Psalter, which contained, besides many new tunes, all that had appeared in Este's Book of Psalms, the practice of naming the tunes was carried to a far greater extent than in any previous collection.

Ravenscroft shall furnish us with one more tune to which his name is attached. His Psalter was so great an improvement upon preceding ones, and has been re-printed so many times, that it cannot fail to be interesting to the historical student. A harmonized version of this tune, with the air given to the treble in accordance with modern usage, is to be found in the Bristol Tune-book—a Tune-book, by the way, which does credit to local talent and local enterprize. The tune is set to a metrical version of the 137th Psalm.

The last year of the 16th century saw an attempt (10) to popularize in this country the placing of the melody in the treble, but I do not find it met with much success.

Scotland had not been without her Psalter, and, like our own country, did not rely solely upon native skill, but drew largely from foreign sources; this, considering where the Reformation commenced, and remembering, too, how song-ful its leader was, is not to be wondered at. The first Scotch Psalter was published in 1566 as far as I can gather, but copies are rare and I have not seen one; the melody only was given. In 1633 another Psalter appeared, with some of the tunes harmonized, and in 1635 Andro Hart published his, giving the whole of the Psalms harmonized in four and five parts. The Reverend Neil Livingstone re-published this edition of Hart's, in 1864, with a most elaborate introduction. He gives in an appendix a few of the tunes from the edition of 1633, and from this I give one example, "The Martyre's Tone." It is needless for me to dwell upon the heroic courage of the Covenanters, or to remind you of the inestimable privileges which the English, as well as the Scotch now enjoy, because of the determined opposition of these brave men to State interference with private religious convictions and worship. The persecution to which the Scotch Protestant Church was subjected in the 16th century, will be an eternal disgrace to the English ecclesiastical authorities of the time, and the melodies which inspired these men, of whom the world was not worthy, must have an abiding interest to all who earnestly seek after truth, and who are therefore presumedly ready to pay that tribute of admiration which fortitude, like that of the Covenanters, deservedly calls for.

---

(10) Richard Allison's "Psalms of David in meter," 1599. This is a very curious production; it gives the letters (after an old notation,) C, D, e, a, &c.

58

The reformed church of Scotland rejected the use of instrumental music in public worship, and to this day organs are looked upon with extreme disfavour; as liberal opinions prevail—as prevail they must—this noble instrument will no longer be contemptuously called a "box o' whistles!" As an interesting relic of the time when the melody was always in the tenor, it is deserving of notice that a *male* voice still leads the psalm in the Scotch Presbyterian Church.

It has been said that Scotch music scarcely admits of any other harmony than a simple bass. Dr. Franklin says of it, "It will last for ever, because the melody is harmony." To understand this, we must bear in mind that melody is a succession of agreeable sounds, and harmony the co-existence of such; when, therefore, the old Scotch melodies, in which every succeeding emphatical note is a third or an octave, or some note connected with the preceding note, were played on the national harp, (the wires of which gave a *continuous* sound,) a good idea of harmony was obtained, for to a certain extent several sounds were concurrent.

The Scottish nation was not imbued throughout with that earnest religious fervour which distinguished the Covenanters, and profane ballads were frequently to be heard. The music of these, as well as of many of the national airs, were set at various times to "Godlie Songs and Hymns." One Robert Wedderburne was rather noted for adaptations of this sort, and his example was recently followed in this country, at the time of the revival a few years ago.

Contemporaneous with the psalm-tune writing of the 16th and 17th centuries must be noticed the great number of Madrigals that were composed; dramatic music was also cultivated, and met with a large amount of success. These necessarily prepared the way for a revolution in sacred music, and the simple melody of the Church Tune gave way to an elaborate style which once more took the hymn from the congregation and gave it to the choir. But a power in the state which had first made itself manifest in the reign of Elizabeth, now threatened to throw the nation, so far as music and classical literature were concerned, back into its condition of the dark ages. The Protestant Church of England had, at its formation, men of all shades of opinion within her fold, and it was natural that the compromise effected by Cranmer between the Church and the State should have proved distasteful to some. These, in the words of Macaulay, "considered it as an attempt to unite the worship of the Lord with the worship of Baal." During the reign of Mary many of these men retired to Switzerland, where, if possible, they strengthened themselves yet further in their hatred of Erastianism and Popery. The persecutions and cruelties of Mary no doubt had a great deal to do with the confirmation of these views, and at her death this party determined to leave no attempt untried to obtain for the Church the right of governing her own affairs, and to get that right vested in their own special section of it. But this they found impossible; Elizabeth was uncompromising, and not one tittle of her prerogative as head of the Church, would she resign. Bent upon attaining their ends, the Puritans often brought themselves within reach of the law, but persecution only added to their desire for a democratical form of government for the Church, a desire for a democratical form of government in political affairs as well, and thus commenced that opposition to the crown which now, a hundred years later, resulted in the establishment of the Commonwealth.

Hitherto the best art, whether musical, architectural, or poetical, had been religious art; the greatest genius had always devoted its best efforts to the service of the church, but now, art was told to take its departure, for the utilitarian view of worship could not co-exist with the more naturally imaginative. To quote a great

---

(11) James Martineau, in his preface to "Hymns for the Christian Church and Home," (Longman, 1869.) The whole of this preface is worth reading.

philosopher of the present day, (11) "The Puritans pressed the fatal question, what was the use of all these glorious symbols, inasmuch as He who is a spirit can take no pleasure in material forms, and the Being whose presence swells the midnight heavens, could see nothing fair in any temple made with hands. Art instantly took flight at the suggestion, and the grandeur and harmony of religion shewed themselves no longer in the form of worship, but rather in the actual life of this class of men."

In Elizabeth's time, the Puritans had complained of the playing on organs, curious singing, &c., and now they petitioned Parliament "that all Cathedral music may be put down where the service of God is grievously abused by piping with organs, singing, ringing, and trowling of psalms from one side of the choir to the other, with the squeaking of chanting choristers." In 1643 therefore, the Puritans having a majority in the House, the Cathedral service was suppressed, and nothing but syllabic and unisonous psalmody was allowed in church. The Directory was substituted for the Book of Common Prayer, and the people were enjoined to make no responses, save the "Amens." On all sides organs were taken down, and the music books destroyed. The chanting of the Psalms was considered too Romish, and this also was discontinued; the dislike to it which characterized Calvin, has ever since been shared by all Calvinistic congregations. The restoration of a revised Book of Common Prayer in Charles the Second's time, revived chanting in the Established Church, but it is only of late years its use has been sanctioned by Dissenters. During the Protectorate two or three plain-tune psalters (containing no harmonies) were published. (12)

1660 saw the restoration of the monarchy, and with it a return once more to elaborate music. While the music in this country had

---

(12) The Revd. Neil Livingstone says, "The Puritan party, though objecting to much of the Cathedral service, does not seem to have had any scruples respecting the attachment of harmony to the psalm tunes."

been lying under a ban, on the Continent, especially in France and Italy, it had been thriving vigorously. Charles and his courtiers found England, as Mr. Hullah says, "wanting in pipes and strings, and in people to play on them." The severe school of Tallis, Bird, Morley, and Orlando Gibbons, suited not their foreign tastes, so musicians from Italy were sent for, and their style of singing was encouraged; this, together with the introduction of the Opera into England in this reign, had a great effect upon the national psalmody. Besides importing artists from abroad however, many young men were sent to Paris at the country's expense, to study under Lulli and other masters; on their return these were appointed to posts in the King's chapel and elsewhere. Pelham Humphries was one such; in three years he was paid £400.

It was some years before all the anticipated results were obtained. Mace, writing in 1676 says, "In most quires there is but one man to a part, and few of them are masters of the art of song." But the fashion was set, and the result coud have been foretold. Mace complains of the Psalms being "tortured and tormented" to such a degree, as rendered it impossible to sing for any length of time, steadily and perfectly in tune, without the aid of some instrument. He mentions one redeeming feature at York-Minster; we will hope it was the custom elsewhere, though from the way in which the incident is noted, it is like hoping against hope. Mace tells us that "the whole congregation there sang a psalm with the choir and organ always before the sermon" (by psalm, meaning of course, a metrical version of one). Of the many Tune-books which continued to be published, John Playford's "Psalms and Hymns" of 1691, is worth mentioning, as here, for the first time, the music was divided into bars, thus enabling it to be sung in regular and understood time. In his preface he says, "The common tunes," (by this he means the plain-song or air,) "are all printed in the tenor part and with the base, and to have this music more full and solemn, I have composed to these, two other parts, viz. two contra-tenors." These latter parts are called in the body of the work, altus and contra-tenor. Church music underwent a great change at the close of this century; the dramatic style introduced at the wish of Charles, could not but materially affect the previous solemn church style,—a style of which Burney said, "It was all of the true church stamp, harmony wonderful, labour distressing, effect in general grave and sedate, sometimes solemn, but exhibiting nevertheless a total want of design, subject, melody, and attention to the accent and meaning of the words." Though anything but perfection therefore, it was certainly to be preferred before the refined songs and operatic airs, which now, alas! were introduced. The congregational hymns were first "tolerated for the sake of the ignorant and weak,"—then abandoned altogether in favour of choir and solo-singing. The introduction of the Italian opera indirectly led to the final giving of the melody to the treble. Eunuchs had lately been employed in Italy to sing the upper part, and their range of voice being greater than that of ordinary men, composers were in consequence enabled to write music higher. When, therefore, these singers came over to England, they had it pretty much their own way, for the practice of singing had greatly fallen off during the Puritanic reign, and high-tenor voices were not only scarce, but their quality was deteriorated. The falsetto of the bass voice was tried as a substitute, but with no pleasing effect, and as there was thus a lack of men's high voices to sustain the accompanying harmonies, the melody would seem to have been given in process of time, to the highest part—the other voices taking their natural places under.

The English Glee dates its rise from this time. There sprang up a general love for delicate part-music written for a *few* voices, and in a short period scarcely a village in England was without its Glee

Club. The difficulty of the music of the 16th century is a clear proof of an extensive cultivation of singing. The frequent allusions to it in the literature of the time, bear out this inference. The art of reading music formed a part of common education, and even charity boys received regular instruction in it. Such a rage for Glee music could not fail to produce *its* effect also upon the music of the church, and Burney assures us the effect of the church service in use in his time, was very different from the solemn effect of that instituted by Tallis, of whose harmonized edition of Marbeck's Book of Common Prayer, he so highly speaks. Arthur Bedford, Vicar of Temple Church of this city, (1711) complained that "our present composers have too much of briskness, and little seriousness left." The plain chant which Marbeck set to the Te Deum was of course not tolerated after the Restoration, and this hymn was soon set to regular services ; nearly every organist writing one or more such. The Te Deum however, because of the ever-varying spirit of its verses, taxed their powers severely ; it would seem as though the perfect rendering of its meaning needed its expansion into a lengthy composition, such as Handel's Dettingen Service, for there is hardly one setting with which serious faults may not be found. The hymn itself is long, and to allow the pauses which its many subjects demand, would doubtless occupy too much time ; but no excuse can atone for the total want of reverence and dignity which characterizes nearly all the early arrangements, and many of the recent ones. The Revd. Edward Young, of Clifton, writing on this subject, but with particular reference to two services—Dr. Aldrich's in G., and Dr. Boyce's—says, "There is in them a consequent uniform continuousness, with a total absence of sensible pauses; from 'We praise Thee, O God,' to 'we therefore pray Thee,' each verse varies in sentiment ; yet these nineteen verses are sung antiphonally with not a single suspension of syllabic sound."

Nearly every Church composer makes the serious blunder of marking the words "praise Thee,"—after "the glorious company of the apostles," (and in the kindred passages also)—with a *forte*, overlooking the fact that the whole sentence is a simple narration of what is taking place elsewhere.

The hymn itself is essentially the people's, yet how seldom can it be sung by them! Of course it is not contended that worship consists solely, or even chiefly, in verbally singing praises to God, yet it must be confessed that the people *ought* to join in *this* universal hymn.

A short movement from Purcell's unpublished Te Deum for Saint Cecilia's Day, is given below as a specimen of the fugal and ornate mode in which a great deal of the Church Music of that period was written; there is no double bar at the close, but the voices immediately, without any pause, go on to the next phrase— the bass indeed, entering it with a passing note in the last bar of this movement.

About the middle of the 17th century the' teachings of John Wesley had taken firm root in this country. Wesley doubtless knew of the immense benefit the employment of psalmody had been to Luther and other Reformers, and he eagerly availed himself of the same means of propagating his views. Both he and his brother Charles wrote a large number of hymns, and these were sung to favourite and popular tunes; fond of music themselves, they succeeded in instilling into the hearts of their followers the same love of psalmody they themselves possessed, and to this day an ardent love of singing—hearty and congregational—is an understood characteristic of Wesleyans.

But the music of the Non-Conforming Churches suffered from the introduction of the dramatic style as much, perhaps more, than that of the Established Church. This latter had an ancient church style, the tradition of which she could not entirely ignore; the Dissenting bodies, however, had no such memories, hence their psalmody drifted into a style which has been described as "rude and shouting."

I have selected two tunes as illustrative of this wretched taste. They are taken from no provincial collection, but from a Tune-book published by a London minister for use in his own and other chapels. The words are Dr. Rippon's own appointing, being printed with the music. The first tune—Lambeth—is written for three voices and is exceedingly lively, while the sentiment of the hymn is just the reverse. The poet describes himself as

"Encompass'd with clouds of distress,
 Just ready all hope to resign,"

and adds he is disheartened, and can only plaintively pour out his song.

Dr. Rippon's Tune-book went through several editions, and many of the tunes contained in it, such as "Westbury Leigh," "Miles' Lane," and others, are still to be heard in those chapels round which old associations still linger. The present generation, however, has, as a rule, discarded these old melodies, and frequently the change has *not* been for the better! T. Walker wrote for this Tune-book an introduction to Psalmody, in which the various musical notes and signs are explained; he tells how to sing grace notes, and also how to attain to the trill or shake.

The second example is from the same book, and is written for four voices; the words are joyous and hopeful, and the music does not belie them, but it would puzzle a modern congregation to keep up with any choir who might select this tune. It must not however, be supposed that such tunes did not "go" in those days; the airs were doubtless well known, and the people joined heartily, at least in the chorus.

Such music carries in itself its own condemnation; no sooner did a deeper reverence for divine things—begotten by a more spiritual religion—prevail, than the incongruity of associating sacred words to music like this, made itself manifest.

To the Oxford movement, which has since culminated in the Anglican party in the church, doubtless belongs the credit of restoring to Psalmody its proper dignity, for this movement was essentially a calling up of the past to re-invigorate, (or rather supplant ?) the present. With the restoration of Church Vestments and long-disused Liturgies, came also a return to the music of the Ancient Church; which music was certainly far preferable to the dance-tunes and secular airs then so generally in use. From that time commenced a reform in Psalmody; composers and compilers alike were careful to select suitable tunes, and it was generally agreed that *as a rule* the old plan of a syllable to a note and a note to a syllable was the best which could be adopted.

Indebted as we are to Germany for important truths, resulting from the exercise of free thought in theological matters, we are indebted to her also for the Chorale which has been our best model for a congregational tune.

Macaulay—when expressing his wonder that Milton, (who himself said he was born an age too late,) should have written so sublimely as he did in that comparatively modern period of English civilization—says it is in the early years of a people, before particularity is lost in generalization, that their language is best adapted for the poet's use. He adds, the same must be said of music, painting, and sculpture.

It is in certain moods of national life, and under certain conditions only, that Psalmody, destined to live for ever, bursts forth.

Though new tunes are continually being dedicated by their composers to the service of the Church, few equal, and none excel the simple, but at the same time grand, melodies of the early German and English schools. An example of a thoroughly good English tune, is that known as the "Evening Hymn." Tallis wrote the original, as we have already seen, for a hymn of sixteen lines, four syllables in each line; Ravenscroft afterwards altered it to suit a long-metre hymn, and also changed the accent. It will now be shown as arranged and harmonized by Mr. Hopkins in his "Temple Tune book." (13)

(13) This Tune-book is a valuable one for musical students. It is divided into three parts; the first comprising old English tunes prior to 1750, the second consisting of foreign, and the third of modern English, tunes.

As an example of a *modern* tune, my friend Mr. Hain (see note to page 76) has kindly allowed me to print his tune "Frankfort." I think it will be generally agreed that it is an excellent specimen of what church tunes should be—simple yet pleasing, and admirably adapted to bring out the meaning of the words to which it is set.

But it is not the hymn-tune only that has undergone modifications. During the last few centuries the Gregorian Chant has failed to satisfy the requirements of Church musicians, so first the single, then the double Anglican Chant was written.

In three or four psalms, such for instance as we find appointed for the morning and evening service in the English Church, a Gregorian, or even a single Anglican Chant would become wearisome from its monotonousness, and the practice of changing the chant for each psalm had its disadvantages. A double chant, however, lessens the number of times the same music is sung just one half, and is consequently less wearisome, while it allows a greater flow of melody. To my mind nothing exceeds the fitness of a good double chant as the vehicle of such poetry as the Church usually appoints to be sung.

A friend (14) who has written a great deal of Church Music, has kindly allowed me to use one of his chants as an example. I think it will be agreed that it is an immense advance upon Gregorians. Jeremy Collier said, "A Church Tune should be a holy thing, fit for a seraph to sing, and an angel to hear."

(14) Mr. William Hain, Junr., of Clifton, who reserves to himself exclusively the copyright of this chant, and also of the tune "Frankfort," on page 75.

A lecture on Church Music would be scarcely complete were no allusion made to the diversities of opinion as to the style best adapted for the purposes of public worship. There are those, who—either skilful in the art themselves, or keenly appreciative of the creations of others—insist upon the necessity which exists for incorporating in the service of the sanctuary the best productions possible. These urge, and with strong reason, that nothing but our best should be given to the Almighty; consequently they would introduce elaborate music, such as the people could not join in, and which therefore would have to be performed by a choir.

There are also those who object thus to worship God by proxy. If, say they, the Church appoints the Te Deum to be said or sung at morning service, with what reason does a paid choir take the words " *We* praise Thee O God " out of our mouths ? It is essentially a hymn for the whole congregation, and it is irreverent to allow one's own thankfulness or deep needs to be expressed by some hired singers ; while the nature of the Being to whom such notes are addressed, must, if truly contemplated, so fill the worshipper with solemn awe as to make the present mode appear an incongruous mockery.

To come to a right understanding on the matter, it is necessary first to know what worship is, and I cannot do better than quote a writer to whom I just now referred. Mr. Martineau says, "Genuine worship is the natural and spontaneous utterance of a mind possessed by the conception of the infinite relations in which we stand, and aspiring towards a point of view worthy of their solemnity."

If this be so—if worship really consists in natural and spontaneous utterances—how *can* that be worship which is done *for one*, in order that it may be done (so it is said) well ? It is evident that the artistic and, let us gladly admit, beautiful forms, when considered *in themselves*, into which so large a part of the Church's service is moulded, cannot be really called worship, for here the form rather than the subject, occupies the prominent place.

I maintain that not one person in a hundred thinks of the various sentiments of the Te Deum as it is being sung by a Cathedral Choir. The very beauty of the form, not to mention lower reasons, effectually distracts the attention from the subject; and if one does feel, what I cannot do better than describe as sentimental—using that word in its *best* sense—the effect is no more than would have been produced had the music alone been heard. The same remark applies of course to anthems; and if it be said it is the conjunction of sacred words with fitting music, and *not* the latter only, which affects one—I reply that frequently the words of the anthem are not to be distinguished, from the manner in which the various voices are arranged to sing, as it were, against each other. Besides, it should be sufficient to remember what power instrumental music *confessedly* has to rouse the passions and excite the feelings.

I quoted Augustine in the early part of this lecture to show how he was touched by the singing of the hymns and canticles in the Church at Milan, but a few years later he censured himself for being so moved with sensual delight in divine worship, and he declares that he often wished "the melodious singing of David's Psalter was moved from his and the Church's ears."

Thomas Aquinas objected to the use of instruments in the service of the Church, for "musical instruments do more stir up the mind to delight, than frame it to a religious disposition, and though under the law such sensitive aid might be needful, under the gospel dispensation there is neither reason nor use for them."

Cornelius Agrippa complained that "the divine offices, holy mysteries, and prayers, are chanted by a company of wanton musicians, hired with great sums of money, not to edify the understanding, but to tickle the ears of their auditory." He justifies the use of such strong language by stating that in consequence of the whining of the descant, the bellowing of the tenor, the barking of the counterpoint, the squeaking of the treble, and the grunting of the bass, "the words cannot be heard." It stands to reason, indeed, that where a company of singers are *paid* to "perform" certain music in public worship—that where a money equivalent is given for their attendance, and the highest bidder secures their services—neither "a natural and spontaneous utterance" nor due reverence are to be found.

If true worship is what Mr. Martineau describes it to be—a voluntary act on our part, prompted by a sense of the relations subsisting between us and the Infinite—how *can* we consistently call that worship which is essentially a vain show?

Master Mace in his "Music's Monument," insists upon all things in the Church being so contrived and ordered that the common, poor, and ignorant people might unite their *voices* as well as their hearts in praising God. He would have all things in the service plain and easy to their capacities. Mace was undoubtedly right. If the fitness of music for the worship of the Great God consisted in its difficulty of execution—if even the beauty of music was inseparable from chromatics, fugues, and canons—then might the plea for an elaborate service be justly made. But such is not the case; the Church possesses a rich store of grand yet simple music; music grand *in its simplicity;* "That which is to stir all Christendom to devotion, is not the elaborate music of the Mass, nor the beautiful strains of a Stabat Mater, but it is the heart-stirring melody of one of our noble hymn-tunes when from '*all* men is out-poured Hallelujah to the Lord;' it is the music which

> 'As for some dear familiar strain,
> Untired we ask and ask again;
> Ever in its melodious store,
> Finding a spell unheard before.'" *

---

* From "The Choir," September 8th, 1866.

The Revd. Neil Livingstone in his preface to "The Scottish Psalter of 1635," says, "Singing in worship should be performed by the body of the people. If music pass beyond the ability of the hearer to join with it vocally, or at least to understand and appreciate its relation to the words, it is apt to be listened to as a performance, and the great ends of worship are forgotten."

That music is best adapted for the service of the Church, which on the one hand is within the ability of average worshippers, and on the other, does not either from its poverty or richness provoke the criticism of a highly cultivated musical taste. The tendency of present thought is towards the abandonment of set forms in which to approach the Creator, and Father of our spirits. Can it be doubted that eventually His creatures, as they grow in spiritual knowledge, will also lay aside as an impediment to the *free* expression of their sentiments, the present confinement of so much of the church's adoration and praise to a "hired company of singers ?"

APPENDIX.

KIESEWETTER says, "Harmony among the Greeks signified a succession of single notes according to their scale, and Melody a succession of these harmonic sounds according to their rules of rhythm. . . . . The first Organ was sent into the Western Country a hundred years after Vitalianus, as a present from the Greek Emperor, Copronymus, to King Pepin."

. . . . "Fauxbourdons was a song of three parts, consisting of a succession of consecutive chords of the $\frac{6}{3}$ in similar motion above the tenor or cantus-fermus, excepting that at the end the highest passed into the octave instead of the sixth, and the end concluded with the chord of the $\frac{8}{3}$. The Fauxbourdon was taken to Rome from Avignon towards the end of the 14th century."

Hawkins writes, "The prodigious havoc and destruction made in the conventual and other libraries at the dissolution of monasteries here, in France, and in Flanders, have left us but few of the compositions from whence a comparison might be drawn between Church Music of this (his) period, and that of earlier times. The few fragments in MS. are totally void of those excellences of succeeding times. The precepts of the science inculcated nothing more than the doctrine of 'counter-point,' and the nature of the canto-fermo; in short, a species of music that knew not length nor duration of sounds."

As having some interest in relation to late discussions as to male-voice singing, I may mention that Hawkins tells us "the [fifth Earl of Northumberland had in his private chapel three basses, three tenors, *six* counter-tenors, and six trebles; these latter being children." The magnificent "style" of this nobleman excited the jealousy of Wolsey, and a requisition was made of the Earl's Music-books!

The ancient scale consisted of four tetrachords of similar form, divided in the middle by a full tone, thus:—

The Gregorian scale omits the highest and lowest of these tetrachords as unsuitable for unisonous singing. The so-called Gregorian Tones are formed from the new scale, thus—

The Ambrosian Tones take the final note from the lower, and the dominant from the higher tetrachord, avoiding B as a dominant from its supposed ambiguity (the Ancients *felt* the semitone). For the Gregorian Tones a lower dominant simply is used—this constituting the sole difference. I give a table of the eight tones, initialing them with the first of the "rising" notes (the starting note) and the dominant; the final cadence originally returned to the starting note, but many of the tones have various endings, and but few now end on the note on which they commenced; while most of them lack two or three of the rising notes.

First Tone (Ambrosian).

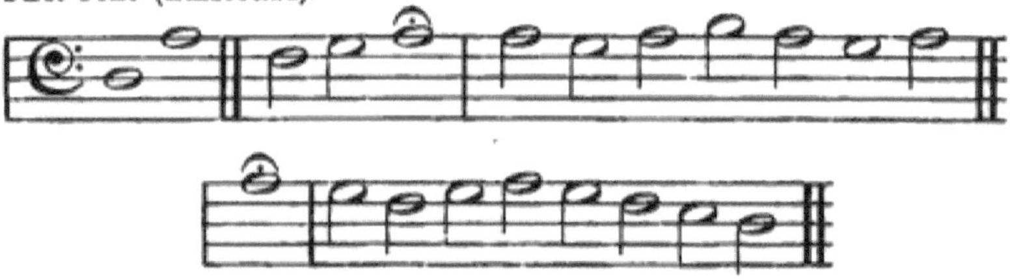

Second Tone (Gregorian).

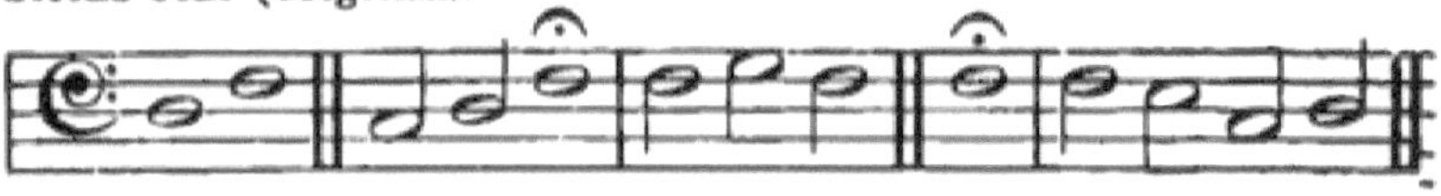

Third Tone (Ambrosian).

iii.

Fourth Tone (Gregorian).

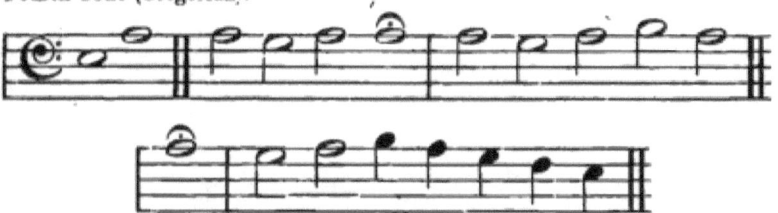

Fifth Tone (Ambrosian).

Sixth Tone (Gregorian).

Seventh Tone (Ambrosian).

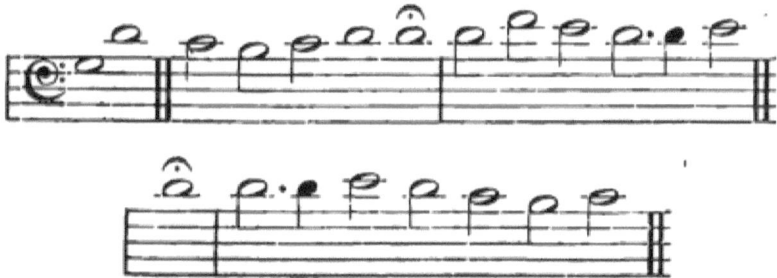

iv.

Eighth Tone (Gregorian).

I have in the text (page 31) given Luther's tune to the 46th Psalm. As it may be interesting to the student of human nature to notice the various responses the musical genius of different nations make to like sentiments, I reprint it here, together with the English tune to the same Psalm, that the two may be compared with each other. "Worms" is here written for four men's voices, and is indeed copied from the German; it would be probably sung in this form on public occasions. The English tune has the melody in the tenor. The harmonies are from the Psalm-singers' Divine Companion, (about 1720) revised by my friend Mr. Callaway.

Worms.

(Harmonized for two Tenors and two Basses.)

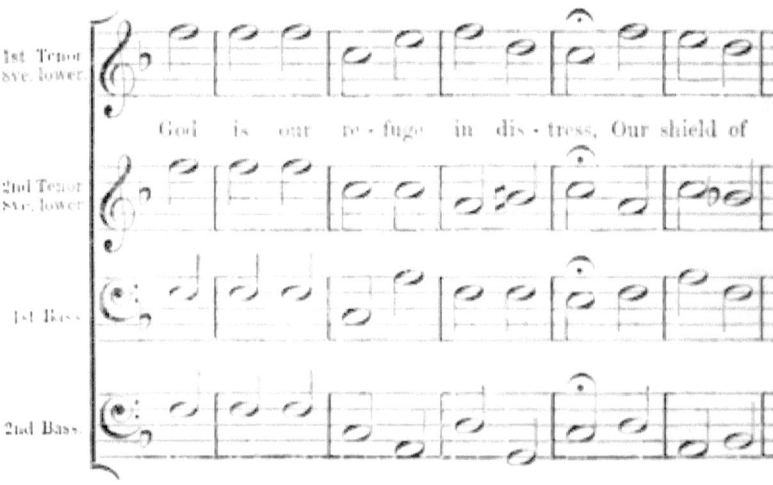

still will we not fear, For Thou, O God, art ev-er near.

46th Psalm.

Daye's Psalter Tune—harmonized.

vii.

The Scottish Psalter adopted the English version, but placed the melody in the Bass, with all the harmonies *above* it. As this was not a very usual custom, and as but few copies of this old Psalter are extant, I have reproduced this setting. Psalmody would be no loser were our organists occasionally to arrange well-known airs in the ancient style, leaving the congregation to sustain the melody (as they would), while the choir sang the descant.

viii.

46th Psalm.

Scottish Psalter, Melody in the Bass.

ix.

TAYLOR BROS., Music & General Printers, Baldwin Street, Bristol.

www.ingramcontent.com/pod-product-compliance
Lightning Source LLC
Chambersburg PA
CBHW021949160426
43195CB00011B/1286